About the workbook

Each of us is a spiritual being who has unique gifts to give to the world. But some of us have not developed this side of ourselves. In this workbook we'll learn about tapping into the goodness at our core to reach spiritual recovery. We'll strengthen our values and our connections with nature, the Twelve Step group, and our Higher Power. We'll learn to use the Twelve Steps and prayer and meditation to improve our daily life and enrich our recovery.

About the author

Lawrence Hyde, M.A., has worked in the fields of chemical dependency and mental health counseling since 1978. Mr. Hyde is the author of *Step Five for Young Adults,* published by Hazelden.

My Spiritual Progress Guide

Keep It Simple Series

by
Lawrence Hyde

 HAZELDEN®

Hazelden
Center City, Minnesota 55012-0176

1-800-328-9000
1-651-213-4590 (Fax)
www.hazelden.org

Editor's note
The Twelve Steps are reprinted with permission of Alcoholics Anonymous World Services, Inc. Permission to reprint the Twelve Steps does not mean that Alcoholics Anonymous has reviewed or approved the contents of this publication, nor that AA agrees with the views expressed herein. The views expressed herein are solely those of the author. AA is a program of recovery from alcoholism. Use of the Twelve Steps in connection with programs and activities that are patterned after AA, but that address other problems, does not imply otherwise.

Hazelden Publishing and Educational Services is a division of the Hazelden Foundation, a not-for-profit organization. Since 1949, Hazelden has been a leader in promoting the dignity and treatment of people afflicted with the disease of chemical dependency.

The mission of the foundation is to improve the quality of life for individuals, families, and communities by providing a national continuum of information, education, and recovery services that are widely accessible; to advance the field through research and training; and to improve our quality and effectiveness through continuous improvement and innovation.

Stemming from that, the mission of this division is to provide quality information and support to people wherever they may be in their personal journey—from education and early intervention, through treatment and recovery, to personal and spiritual growth.

Although our treatment programs do not necessarily use everything Hazelden publishes, our bibliotherapeutic materials support our mission and the Twelve Step philosophy upon which it is based. We encourage your comments and feedback.

The headquarters of the Hazelden Foundation are in Center City, Minnesota. Additional treatment facilities are located in Chicago, Illinois; New York, New York; Plymouth, Minnesota; St. Paul, Minnesota; and West Palm Beach, Florida. At these sites, we provide a continuum of care for men and women of all ages. Our Plymouth facility is designed specifically for youth and families.

For more information on Hazelden, please call **1-800-257-7800.** Or you may access our World Wide Web site on the Internet at **www.hazelden.org.**

WELCOME!

Two friends decide to see a movie. They make their way into a theater. The lights are dimmed, music plays softly, and the smell of buttered popcorn drifts through the air. The two friends talk of small things, as friends will do, while they wait for the show to start. As the movie begins, suddenly one friend turns to the other and says, "Look! They filmed the movie out of focus!"

We know better, of course. Movies are made as close to perfect as possible. If what we see is out of focus, distorted, or flawed, we rightly believe something is wrong with the projector.

When it comes to ourselves, though, we are usually all too ready to believe what we see, hear, and feel. When we have a disease, such as chemical dependency, or when we have thoughts and feelings that cause us problems, we're ready to believe we're flawed or bad. Nothing could be further from the truth.

What It Means to Be a Spiritual Being

The truth is, each of us is a spiritual being first. The word *spiritual* means different things to different people. For our purposes in this workbook, *spiritual* means those qualities, abilities, and attitudes that help us to see that we're more than this body and mind, that at our core we're not flawed or bad.

Over time, we've come to form beliefs, attitudes, and habits that may or may not work for us today. Because of what we've been told or what we've lived through, we may believe we're shameful, bad, lazy, inept, hateful, and so on. The truth is this: We may have been born with a body chemistry that made us more likely to become addicted or ill. When we try to shine the perfect truth of our spiritual being through this imperfect physical body and through the flawed way we think and feel, what comes out is distorted, imperfect, and flawed. How could it be any other way?

Our past training may have shaped our spiritual beliefs. Some of us may believe that when we die, our spiritual part will go on to some

1

afterlife and our bodies and minds will just stop altogether. Some of us may have been taught that we have a soul. But that soul is not us; it's just something that we have, like an appendix or tonsils. It's not really needed; we're just sort of stuck with it. We're left with the idea that we should act and think in certain religious or moral ways to benefit a part of us that we've never seen, can't touch, and will lose anyway when we die.

WHY WOULD WE CARE MUCH ABOUT SPIRITUALITY?

This workbook can help you rethink your beliefs about spirituality. You'll learn ways to approach spiritual recovery that may be new to you. You'll be able to keep close tabs on your progress as you learn more about yourself and life in recovery.

What's Spiritual Recovery?

Now is the time to begin our spiritual "un-covery." After all, that's what this lifelong process of spiritual recovery is all about. It's not necessarily about religion; it's about uncovering the good qualities we have at our core. Instead of feeling that we have to adopt new spiritual qualities, we need to see that we already have these qualities in abundance. We need to form new attitudes, beliefs, and habits that will help us know the truth about ourselves.

Spiritual recovery helps us move toward the truth about ourselves—that we're created perfect and need to let that perfection shine through. Knowing this truth, we can then form new practices, beliefs, and ways of thinking that help us move away from the darkness of addiction and toward the light of recovery.

Spiritual recovery helps us change our thinking and feeling so we're no longer weighted down with feelings of shame, guilt, or fear. We may still feel these things when we make a mistake. But we'll no longer believe that *we* are wrong. Instead, we'll come to see that while we make mistakes, at our very core we're good. This simple idea—that our very nature is good, rather than flawed, evil, or bad—can and will change our view of the world, ourselves, and our lives.

What's Spirituality and Why Should I Want It?

In order to make gains in spiritual recovery, we need to have a sense of what we believe. Knowing just what spirituality is can help. *Spirituality* is anything that helps us to connect with something greater than ourselves in a way that gives us a sense of inner calm. It's made up of three things:

- what we believe about ourselves
- what we're connected to
- what we believe about life

In the sections that follow, we'll look at each of these three things in turn.

What We Believe about Ourselves

If we're going to think of ourselves as spiritual beings, we need to know our spiritual qualities. Anytime we act for the good of another person, anytime we feel love for another person, a group, or a country, anytime we serve others without expecting anything in return, we're showing spiritual qualities.

Name at least one time when you

Showed kindness:

Felt patience:

Were calm:

Helped others:

Prayed to God (or a Higher Power):

Showed caring:

Felt love:

Resisted temptation:

Stuck up for someone else:

Held to what you thought was right:

List several other times when your spiritual qualities have shone through:

What We're Connected To

Many people new in recovery have trouble with the idea of spirituality. Many of us had bad experiences with religion when we were kids, and organized religion may have been the only area in our lives where the word *spiritual* was used.

There are many ways that we can connect with the spiritual. In the exercises that follow, we'll look at some common paths to spirituality. We'll also look at some of the common roadblocks we may face in recovery.

Nature. One person new to recovery lived in a western state. "The mountains—whenever I need to feel in contact again, I just go to the mountains," he said. "Just being there lets me know there's something more, something bigger than me."

Those of us who don't have access to mountains can use other parts of nature for inspiration. Some people swear they feel closest to their God or Higher Power (about which we'll say more later) when they're in the woods, at the seashore, or in the desert. Others connect with their spirituality by watching a sunset, a rainbow, or walking in a gentle spring rain.

What are five parts of nature that have helped you to feel more in touch with others, the world, or yourself?

1.

2.

3.

4.

5.

The Group. Of course nature leaves some people totally cold. They may prefer to use their self-help group as a way to connect with the spiritual. "Twelve people have more power than one person has," is how one man put it. "And at least I don't feel like I'm just talking to myself."

A woman in recovery agreed. "A good meeting takes me out of myself. Sometimes I get to thinking that I'm the only one who has felt a certain way or has had a certain problem. Going to meetings makes me see how much alike we all are."

List four times when going to a self-help meeting has helped you feel more connected with life, other people, or your Higher Power:

1.

2.

3.

4.

Religion. For some of us, religion may have been a positive experience before we ever came to spiritual recovery. Our idea of God may have involved such figures as Jesus Christ, Buddha, or Allah. "This is the God of my childhood," said one person new to recovery. "When they started talking about spirituality, my first thought was to return to the church. In all my troubles, I never felt that God left me; I felt like I left God, and the church."

List three times when going to church, praying in the way that you were taught to pray, or talking to your minister, priest, or rabbi has helped you feel connected with something greater than yourself:

1.

2.

3.

Many of us in recovery run into problems when we try to use God as our connection to spirituality. One reason is that we've come to see ourselves as having failed our religion. Because of our addiction, we may have broken commandments, stopped going to church, or done wrongs we think are unforgivable. Some religions portray God as very strict and demanding; once we have passed a certain point, some religions tell us, we may be damned for all time. Small wonder, then, that the idea of going to church really scares many of us. Guilt, and the belief that our wrongs can never be made right, keep us ashamed and alone.

What are five things you've done that would make it hard for you to return to an organized religion?

1.

2.

3.

4.

5.

Each of us in recovery also lives with the memories of the things we did when addicted. Knowing these things about ourselves, we may think other churchgoers would be shocked if the truth came out. We may think there would be no place among these people for someone who has done the things we've done.

Describe the last time you went to church for a worship service.

If you've never been to a church service, think about what it might be like. Imagine the people who are there to worship.

How do the people around you look and act? What is your frame of mind? Write some of your thoughts here.

The truth is, no matter who we are or what we have become, we are no better or worse than any other person. We are all created perfect. No one is better than anyone else, no matter what we've done. The only difference between us is how much of that underlying perfection we can let shine through. What we show to the world through our actions and attitudes is at best only a fraction of the beauty that lies beneath.

Other Connections. There may be other things we've not covered yet that can help us feel spiritually connected. Some examples are loving and being loved by another person, reading about a great person from the past or about the suffering of a people, and sharing time with a person who inspires us.

List three things (outside of nature, the group, and religion) that have helped you to feel connected to something beyond yourself:

1.

2.

3.

What We Believe about Life

Human beings have always struggled with questions about the meaning of life. Why are we here? What are we supposed to do? What matters?

These questions are big ones for people in recovery. Humans often feel pain, loneliness, or fear when thinking about the meaning of their lives. In fact, it may be that not seeing the meaning in their lives led to taking the first drink or drug.

What we think about the meaning of life often changes as we grow older and gain wisdom. Some of us, however, may come up with one meaning that will satisfy us for the rest of our lives.

In spiritual recovery, we try to answer these questions for ourselves based on what we know and believe now. We need, however, to allow room to change our thinking as we grow in recovery.

Write your answers to the following questions in the spaces provided. If after giving a question a lot of thought you truly don't know what you believe, write what seems most likely to be true.

The universe was created by

Human beings are on earth because

The things I can do that will give my life the most value are

My ideas about the right way to live are based on

The purpose of my life as I see it now is

How will my current ideas about life help or hinder my recovery?

If my ideas about life will not help my recovery, how can I learn other ways of thinking about the meaning and purpose of life?

It's a good idea to review your thinking about yourself, your life, and your Higher Power every six to twelve months. The preceding exercises will help you see how your ideas have changed or confirm that your ideas are still right for you.

Your Higher Power and You

Whenever we talk about being connected to something greater than ourselves, there's always a question: What, exactly, are we connected to? Perhaps nothing in spiritual recovery causes so much confusion, discussion, and argument as the nature of the Higher Power. Some people believe in a Christian God. Agnostics believe we can't prove that God exists and that we cannot know or contact God. Atheists believe there is no God. Some people believe in a force of nature, or a "spirit that moves in all things."

No matter what we believe, it's important that each of us have a meaningful God or Higher Power. Each of us needs a personal, private, and unique relationship with God or a Higher Power.

We don't need to think of the Creator of the universe when we think of God. We don't even need to refer to God at all when we think of a Higher Power. A *Higher Power* is anything greater than ourselves that cares about us and has the power to move us from addiction to recovery.

When we think of a Higher Power, we should remember that we're all equal. No one person is truly greater than another. Trying to make another person—such as a parent, lover, spouse, or minister—our Higher Power is a formula for disaster. Humans can and will let us down, even when they don't want to. A Higher Power must be able to help us each time help is needed. No human can do that.

What's the name of your Higher Power or God?

Can your Higher Power be contacted? Why or why not?

Does your Higher Power care about you? If so, why? If not, why not?

Can your Higher Power move you from addiction to recovery? How?

Can you count on your Higher Power to help you in recovery every time you need help for the rest of your life? Why?

What do you need to do to be on good terms (feel comfortable) with your Higher Power?

If your Higher Power doesn't fit the description previously given, what other Higher Powers can you think of?

My Spirituality: A Summary

We began this section by looking at the three parts of spirituality: what we believe about ourselves, what we're connected to, and what we believe about life. Now we need to bring all three together. Answering the following questions can help.

I am a spiritual being who has shown these spiritual qualities: (See the exercises on pages 3-4.)

Three ways that I can feel connected to something or someone greater than myself are as follows: (See pages 4-9.)

1.

2.

3.

Based on my answers from the exercises on page 11, this is what I believe I can give to and receive from my Higher Power or God:

My three most clear-cut ideas about the meaning or purpose of life, as I understand it now, are as follows:

1.

2.

3.

OUR SPIRITUAL RECOVERY PROGRAM: PUTTING THE PARTS TOGETHER

Earlier we said that the things that help us connect with something greater than ourselves and give us a sense of inner calm are spiritual. Our spiritual recovery program, then, should include actions that help move us toward greater and greater connection with something outside ourselves. We need to try to let more and more of our spiritual qualities show; our recovery program should help us do that. We can start to look at certain things that may help us practice spiritual recovery.

Your spiritual recovery program may contain some or all of the parts listed in this section. Also, you may have some qualities in your program that are unique to you. The idea is not to do exactly what someone else has done, but to actually try out these different activities. Find what works for you, what helps you connect with something outside yourself. Be ready to let go of something if, after giving it an honest try, you find that it's not for you.

What the Twelve Steps Can Do for You

The Twelve Step program of recovery emphasizes spirituality, not just religion. If you have been through formal treatment for your addiction, you likely know about the Twelve Steps. Or you may have learned about them through a recovery group that's based on the Steps.

The Twelve Steps contain all the parts of a sound spiritual recovery program. One Step in particular—Step Four—deals specifically with helping us to know more of the truth about ourselves.

Doing Step Four, we see both the good and the not-so-good points about ourselves. Some of these truths may be hard to swallow. Oddly enough, many of us have had more trouble seeing our good points! But if we're to know ourselves as spiritual beings first, we must be ready to look at all our qualities, good and not so good.

If you haven't done Step Four, this is a good time to start; any number of self-help workbooks can guide you through the Step. Or talk with your sponsor or counselor. **Stop! Don't do the rest of this workbook until you've reviewed your work in Step Four.**

As you reviewed your Fourth Step, how did you feel about yourself?

Think about the list you made in the Fourth Step. You may have listed many times when you did something wrong or harmed other people. Below, write about three times when you helped another person or did something good for someone without thinking of yourself first:

1.

2.

3.

As you think about your Fourth Step now, think about these good actions too. How do you feel about yourself as a person?

How can frequent reviews of your Fourth Step help your spiritual recovery? Perhaps doing the Fourth Step reminds you that you have good qualities; that you're making progress in recovery; that you have work yet to do.

Let's take a look at the Steps that refer to the spiritual part of recovery. Remember, these Steps do not limit you to any particular concept of God or a Higher Power. The writers of the Big Book of Alcoholics Anonymous made that very clear:

> When, therefore, we speak to you of God, we mean your conception of God. This applies, too, to other spiritual expressions which you find in this book. Do not let any prejudice you may have against spiritual terms deter you from honestly asking yourself what they mean to you.*

Beneath each of the Steps that follow, write in your own words how this Step can help your spiritual recovery program. Some examples might include the following: being connected; feeling more calm; getting rid of blocks to letting your spiritual self shine through; and seeing the truth about yourself.

Step Two: *Came to believe that a Power greater than ourselves could restore us to sanity.*

Step Three: *Made a decision to turn our will and our lives over to the care of God as we understood Him.*

Step Five: *Admitted to God, to ourselves, and to another human being the exact nature of our wrongs.*

Step Six: *Were entirely ready to have God remove all these defects of character.*

---

*From *Alcoholics Anonymous* [known as "The Big Book"], 3d ed. (New York: AA World Services, Inc., 1976), 47. Reprinted with permission of AA World Services, Inc.

Step Seven: *Humbly asked Him to remove our shortcomings.*

Step Eleven: *Sought through prayer and meditation to improve our conscious contact with God as we understood Him, praying only for knowledge of His will for us and the power to carry that out.*

Step Twelve: *Having had a spiritual awakening as the result of these steps, we tried to carry this message to others, and to practice these principles in all our affairs.*[*]

Why Should We Pray?

Prayer can be an important part of recovery. Prayer may be as formal as a ceremony with candles, music, and hundreds of people, or as simple as a wordless cry from the heart. Prayer is the opening of ourselves to something greater than ourselves, to something we believe cares about us and wishes to help.

There are many forms of prayer, and there is no one right way to pray. If the *form* of our prayer keeps us from connecting with our Higher Power or God, then we need to find some other form of prayer that works for us.

Some of us are uncomfortable with prayer. This may be because of our early religious training. Or it may be because of the awkwardness we feel trying to talk to God. One way to overcome awkwardness is to pray as if we're talking to an older brother or sister, loving parent, or wise, caring teacher. This puts a naturalness and feeling into our prayers that may otherwise be blocked.

---

[*]Step Twelve is from the Twelve Steps of Al-Anon. Step Twelve of the original Twelve Steps of Alcoholics Anonymous uses the word *alcoholics* rather than *others*. For the complete Twelve Steps of AA, see page 24.

What are some prayers you feel good about?

If you have little or no experience with prayer, try to imagine or feel what a comfortable way of praying might be. Or simply pray and pay attention to any feelings you have.

Name three things that might cause you to feel awkward around prayer (for example, old religious training, not being sure how to pray, lacking faith, being uncertain about the nature of God).

1.

2.

3.

Name three times when praying, or trying to pray, has been a source of comfort or has helped you stay sober:

1.

2.

3.

Meditation

Prayer opens us up to something greater than ourselves; meditation allows that something to contact us. Prayer and meditation are like talking on the telephone: when we pray we talk into the mouthpiece; when we meditate we get quiet so we can listen and hear.

There are many ways to meditate. One way, favored by many people in recovery, is to choose a favorite spiritual phrase or passage from a book or poem. Repeat it several times. Then simply let your mind loose. In this way fresh ideas, understanding, and guidance will sometimes appear. Do this before going to work or school, or just before going to bed.

Meditation exercise. Reread this sentence several times: *Prayer opens us up to something greater than ourselves; meditation allows that something to contact us.* Now, sitting comfortably in a quiet place, allow your mind to consider what you've read. Don't try to force understanding or thoughts. A quiet, daydreaming sort of attitude is best. If your mind wanders too far from what you've read, gently bring your focus back. Allow yourself five to ten minutes to do this exercise.

What new ideas or understanding, if any, did you receive?

1.

2.

3.

Practice this exercise for five to ten minutes twice a day for one week. Use a different thought or idea each time. Again, don't try to force understanding. Sometimes new thoughts will appear; sometimes they won't. The value is in the doing. Learn to let go of your need to direct your thoughts. Allow room for new ways of seeing and doing things, and be open to guidance from your Higher Power.

Our minds tend to be noisy places, filled with the thoughts, images, feelings, and emotions pouring out from our mental computers. To gain spiritual awareness we must quiet these noises for a time. Then we can refocus on something other than the constant chatter going on in our heads.

Bringing our minds to complete silence is hard. Our brains seem to want to chatter all the time. Still, with patience and effort we can get totally quiet for short periods of time. At first these periods of silence may last from ten seconds to several minutes. Yet this is more than enough time for our Higher Power to talk to us.

Another meditation exercise. Sit comfortably in a quiet place. Try to keep your back reasonably straight, but sit comfortably. Close your eyes. Think about a warm, glowing, pure white light about ten feet in front of you. Now, let the glow become brighter and larger as it moves closer and closer to your head. Allow the light to enter and fill your mind. Notice how your thoughts seem to slow down or disappear as you look at the light. Let the light move back away from you for a short time. Notice what happens in your mind. Finish by letting the light fill your mind again. Rest in the silence for a brief time.

What happened in your head when you let the light fill you?

What were your thoughts when you let the light move away?

How did it feel to be filled with light?

What problems, if any, did you have with this exercise?

Practice this exercise at least once a day at first, working your way up to twice a day. If you have trouble getting good pictures in your mind's eye, substitute a single word such as *God, Light,* or *One.* Repeat that word and focus on it. Let the word come and go as you did with the light, and notice what happens to your thoughts.

Becoming comfortable with this type of meditation will take practice and patience. Your mind will wander, especially at first. Don't worry. This happens to everyone who tries it. When your mind wanders, gently bring your focus back to the light or the word. Your focus will be better on some days than it is on others.

What you will gain from this type of meditation are brief periods of stillness. In these periods of stillness, your Higher Power doesn't have to compete with any other thoughts to get your attention. You may receive from your Higher Power words, phrases, images, or sounds. Simply note whatever you receive, and think about it after your meditation is over.

In time, no matter what type of meditation you do, try to work up to at least twenty minutes twice a day. This gives your Higher Power many chances to get past the chattering in your mind and to give you understanding and guidance.

Step Eleven Can Give Us Knowledge and Guidance

When we pray for knowledge of God's will for us, and when we open ourselves to guidance, we're doing Step Eleven. Very few of us will ever receive a blueprint of our purpose in life. Most of us are grateful for a hint, a word or phrase, or a sense of inner knowledge that answers at least some of our questions.

One final word about receiving guidance. Often we may be guided into performing a certain action, making changes in our lives, or thinking a certain way. But when we try to put the guidance we receive into practice, we may find that the path is blocked. This may confuse us; after all, aren't we doing what we're supposed to do?

The problem lies in the idea of spiritual time versus physical time. We tend to believe that we're given the guidance we need right now (physical time). In fact, we may be given guidance we will need a week, month, year, or decade from now (spiritual time). The results of that guidance in our lives may not be obvious for a very long time.

If we think we should do something about the guidance we've received through our meditation and prayer, we should do it. If we run into obstacles, we need to pray and meditate for understanding. We also need to know when enough is enough and when we can get on with some other part of our lives.

Finally, some of us may be confused about whether it's OK to pray for things or blessings for ourselves or others. This is largely a matter of personal belief and practice. But when we practice Step Eleven, our task is clearly to pray and meditate only for the knowledge of God's will and the power to carry it out.

Self-Help Groups Help You Feel Connected

Meetings of self-help groups such as Alcoholics Anonymous, Al-Anon, and Sex and Love Addicts Anonymous can be a big support for us. Some of us think that the fellowship and acceptance found in these meetings are the main things that encourage recovery. "Keep coming back," we hear people say at meetings. "It gets better."

Self-help groups can be one part of our program of spiritual recovery. Remember, *spirituality* is anything that helps us connect with something greater than ourselves in a way that gives us a sense of inner calm. The question, then, is whether we feel both connected and more calm after our meetings.

Self-help groups vary a great deal in how well they help us. The exercise that follows is designed to tell you if the group you attend is likely to help you feel connected and more calm. (If you haven't gone to self-help group meetings, save this exercise for later.) Answer yes or no to the following statements:

	Yes	No
I really look forward to my self-help meetings.	_____	_____
When I walk into the meeting place, I feel as if I belong.	_____	_____
I feel "connected" to at least two people in my group.	_____	_____
The mood of most people at my meeting is usually positive.	_____	_____

	Yes	No
My group allows each person to take turns chairing meetings.	_____	_____
My group rarely spends a lot of time going over the same old things without getting anywhere.	_____	_____
I feel free to talk about myself or to respond to others without fearing that they will find fault.	_____	_____
Several times at meetings someone has said exactly what I needed to hear.	_____	_____
When I leave my meeting I usually feel better or more calm.	_____	_____
There have been several times when I've felt closer to my Higher Power after a meeting.	_____	_____

If the answer to more than three of these questions is no, then your group may not be meeting your needs as well as it could. It's important that you give your self-help group a fair chance. But if the group isn't meeting your needs, you might think about going to a different group, one that will help rather than hinder your spiritual recovery.

Remember, spiritual recovery is about letting the perfection of our true selves shine through. Being weighted down with doubt, fear, or anger because of our self-help meetings will not help us achieve spiritual recovery.

Religion

Organized religion has already been discussed at some length. If you feel comfortable attending a particular church, and if by going to church you feel connected to something greater than yourself, then attending church *will* aid your spiritual recovery.

However, if you feel filled with guilt, shame, or doubt each time you attend church, you may wish to consider either attending a different church (perhaps within the same faith) or not attending church at all while you come to terms with yourself and your God. Your pastor or minister may be able to help you sort through your confusion. Your sponsor may also be a good person to talk with if you have concerns.

As a last resort, you may wish to consider searching for a new religion or faith. However, exploring new faiths can cause doubt and confusion also. Go slow, and be sure to have someone trustworthy to talk with about your new ideas and questions.

In what ways will going to church aid your spiritual recovery?

In what ways will it hinder your spiritual recovery?

Name three persons you can talk with if you have concerns about the effect of going to church on your spiritual recovery:

1.

2.

3.

NOW WE CAN MOVE ON TOWARD THE LIGHT

By now we have uncovered a simple truth about ourselves: We are created perfect with many good spiritual qualities, and it is our nature to express them. Our spiritual recovery will help us live out that truth. It is based on a three-step process. First, we'll learn the truth of ourselves. Second, we'll connect with something greater than ourselves. And third, we'll learn to live our lives in a way that gives us a sense of inner calm.

Spiritual recovery is something we can do the rest of our lives. No one reaches the point of fully realizing this spiritual nature and living that nature all the time. Still, even small gains in realizing our own spirituality move us away from the pain and darkness of our addiction and toward the light inside us.

THE TWELVE STEPS OF ALCOHOLICS ANONYMOUS*

1. We admitted we were powerless over alcohol—that our lives had become unmanageable.

2. Came to believe that a Power greater than ourselves could restore us to sanity.

3. Made a decision to turn our will and our lives over to the care of God *as we understood Him.*

4. Made a searching and fearless moral inventory of ourselves.

5. Admitted to God, to ourselves, and to another human being the exact nature of our wrongs.

6. Were entirely ready to have God remove all these defects of character.

7. Humbly asked Him to remove our shortcomings.

8. Made a list of all persons we had harmed, and became willing to make amends to them all.

9. Made direct amends to such people wherever possible, except when to do so would injure them or others.

10. Continued to take personal inventory and when we were wrong promptly admitted it.

11. Sought through prayer and meditation to improve our conscious contact with God *as we understood Him,* praying only for knowledge of His will for us and the power to carry that out.

12. Having had a spiritual awakening as the result of these steps, we tried to carry this message to alcoholics, and to practice these principles in all our affairs.
